flower

ALSO BY JAY WALKER

Where I'm Coming From

Sifting through the Ashes of Me

flower

jay walker

The Merry Blacksmith Press

2011

Flower

© 2011 Jay Walker

For information, address:

The Merry Blacksmith Press
70 Lenox Ave.
West Warwick, RI 02893

merryblacksmith.com

Published in the USA by The Merry Blacksmith Press

ISBN— 0-61556-627-8
978-0-61556-627-6

Dedicated to
Isis Storm,
Nancy Schoenewolf Foley
& all the women who
inspire me to be
a better man.

Table of Contents

Poet, Know Thy Power

I'm tired of hearing people say that poetry
  doesn't save lives
I'm even more tired of hearing it
  from other poets
A person who thinks this is true
   has never held razor to wrist even tentatively
     never held the lip of an open pill bottle
      to the lip of an open mouth
  looking to fill the void of one with the other
     the void of an empty soul
  which is not the same as a lack
        as a simple nothingness
        as simply not being full
  but the void of a vacuum sucking the life from you
    the void of a sucking chest wound festering
       of a claw ripping out a piece of you
      an empty soul
     is still bursting full of pain
     aching for a release
A person who thinks poetry doesn't save lives
  doesn't know the wonders
    a warm embrace can work
  doesn't know how good
    even a gentle pat can feel
  doesn't understand the magic
    in a touch from someone
      when you thought no one was even there
  doesn't realize that words have arms outstretched
    ready to wrap around everyone
     even the writer
     especially the writer

Poetry doesn't save lives?
Poet, mind your tongue!
Whether you believe
      in the structured, formed language
           of "Let there be Light"
      or the more primitive
            guttural
            basic blare of a Big Bang
          it was still sound that sent things spinning
             still the *spoken* idea
         that brought things about
Poet, words have power
Sticks & stones may break one's bones
      but words have built
            & destroyed
            & rebuilt reputations
                nations
                worlds
                entire universes
         words have made some into leaders
           & inspired others to truly lead
         words have shared ideas
            that brought some to greatness
              & others to utter ruin
         words have given hope to those
            with no other reason to go on
         words can do all this
            so how can they not
               have the power to save lives?

I know
I love
I respect the power of words
I use that power liberally
I choose those words carefully

I treat that gift responsibly
    making sure to never waste it
        never abuse it
        or misues it
    but never hide it
      never hold it back
   & never
     ever
        deny its power
Poet
You are a wordsmith
    building the ideas that shape worlds
      in the fires of our souls
      & the forges of our minds
Poet
    know thy power
I know my power
I know the power of words
I know they change lives
I know they save lives
I know
    they've saved mine.

Prince Charming, He Is Not

A roomful of people more shallow than most puddles
      can leave a heart more arid than the Sahara
Sitting in a crowded room, physically,
      but your mind wanders the desert of your soul
The bartender keeps your throat quenched
      but you're still thirsty for something … else
How about this tall drink of water that just
      glided through the door?
His eyes are an oasis of unfathomable depths
      & you are left drunk by their cognac hue
               blinded by the shine in his smile
               lulled by his smooth, soothing voice
               swayed by his swagger & stance
He is music to your snake ears
      & you are charmed as never before
How you long to feel those soft lips trace
      every inch of you
               like two explorers, Lewis & Clark,
      following the path to your Louisiana Purchase
How you yearn to feel his mouth & hands
      discover your territory
               making you ache & shiver & quake
      until you can no longer wait
               to take every last inch of him inside you
               make him one with you
               make him love you
But be careful of this tall, dark & handsome stranger
You think this is your knight in shining armor
      riding his majestic steed
               & rescuing you from the dungeon of loneliness
He is not

He is as refreshing as the glass of water
       & as temporary
Those who build their worlds around him
       will imprison him
When he breaks free, he will destroy you
       'though it's the last thing he would want to do
So heed this warning:
Do not look for the answers in his eyes
       for his soul is full of questions,
             more so than yours
Do not build him a pedestal
       upon which he will not stand
Do not be lulled by the music in his voice alone
       but listen to the lyrics,
             for they say what he is
I'm like a bird; I'll only fly away ...
       & though his love is rare
       & though his love is true
           a day will come
           when he must fly
               break the bonds of his birth place
           & find his spirit's true home
Do not mistake him for Prince Charming ...
       he is not
He is just a man
       & not quite that yet
           & in searching for adulthood
                     for his soul
                     for his salvation
                     for himself
             he will leave you behind
Do not misunderstand what I say
This is no simple statement of "stay away"

No, reach for him, if you dare
        but be aware
He longs for connection like an Internet junkie
Just realize that there comes a time in everyone's life
        when he must sign off
So, go to him, if you want him
      know him
      be with him
      love him
            but learn to let him go.

What Happened?

What happened here?
What happened to us?
How could we have let this happen
   when we knew how to avoid it all along?
What happened to Up With People?
What happened to Hands Across America?
When did singing "We Are The World"
   become passé, even corny?
Why is "Do They Know It's Christmas?"
   now so "eighties"?
Why can't it be Christmas everyday
      everywhere
     to everyone?
What happened to "Give Peace A Chance"?
What happened to "Make Love, Not War"?
& what *is* so funny 'bout peace, love & understanding?
What happened to the dream, Martin?
Are you listening
  watching
   witnessing the hard work you wove
 into the very fabric of this country
   unravel before thousands of crying eyes?
What happened to the Golden Rule?
What happened to "Love thy neighbor as thyself"?
What happened to the teachings of Christ
      the word of God
       Allah
       Buddha?

What happened to the Wiccan Rede?
What happened to our faiths?
What happened to our faith?
What happened to our saviors
         our messiahs
         our leaders
         our prophets?
Why do we keep killing the ones
    who hold the truth in their hands?
Why do we keep killing
When will it stop, when we're *all* dead?
What happened to empathy?
What happened to compassion?
What happened to plain ol'
     common sense
       sensibility
       sensitivity to others?
What happened to love?
Where did it go?
Was it killed a little more
    with the death of each new messenger it sent
      or is it still inside us somewhere
        banging against the doors of our hearts
        begging to be let out?

Huh?
Can you tell me, please?
I'm begging you,
    can anyone answer my questions?
What happened to love?
What happened to us?
   & what happens
       next?

She Is

She is no soldier, made to follow orders,
    I no general to give them
She is no radio with remote control,
    I have not in m hand
        the power to change her tune or turn her off
She is no dog to keep on a leash,
    though she may be a bitch sometimes,
        when she feels justly provoked
She is no vicious circus cat
    meant to cower at the crack of my whip-tongue
She is no Kate, nor I Pertruccio,
    or I am, in that I realize
        the shrew needs not be tamed,
        but merely loved
She is no slave, nor I her master
She is no employee, nor I her boss
She is no child, nor I her parent
She is her own person
  has her own feelings
  has her own way of expressing them
  has the right to do so
I …
We have no right to think otherwise
You have the right to love it
        like it
        loathe it
  but let her know it

Otherwise,
    you also have the right
      to remain silent.

Nobody's Home

I told you before how I wanted to be naked
        but the breeze from scorecards flung up
             is cold against my skin
I wanted to lay my armor down
        but publishers' pens prove mightier than swords
I wanted to tag my name on your blank-wall expression
        but I can't tell if my words are sticking
Is your brain washing clean the minute I stain you?
You have that glossed-eye look
Are my scissor-sayings cutting through
      the red tape of your soul
           or do you find them too dull?
My pencil leads are bullets
      & your heart wears Kevlar
My points are not hollow
      but I still can't get through
I am calling on my digital soul phone
      but I can't seem to find a connection
I am the Babe
    the Hammer
      McGuireSosaBonds swingin' to knock your senses
        out of Complacency Park
    but I can hear the
      whiff-whiff-whiff
        between your ears
     & my scores are strikes against me

I long to go the distance
        but this race is a sprint & I'm pressed for time
                while others run this course in under 3 minutes
My body is a milk carton
My soul is missing & I'm searching through your eyes
        hoping I'm not John Walsh looking for Adam
Notice I haven't used a TV metaphor
It's because I want to do more than just entertain you
                I seek to actually *raise* your IQ
                I want to take the blindfold off
                        give you the antidote
                        wake you from your coma
I want to get you up out of your bed
        have you run to your door
                throw it wide &
                streak naked down your streets
I want to see you
I want *you* to see *me*
I want to see you see me, see?
So, here I am, banging down your door
        but you don't answer
Your shades are drawn
        I can't even see through your windows
Is anybody home?
Damn,
        now I know how a Jehovah's Witness feels.

Save Me

Dear Wonder Woman:
I don't know the male counterpart to "damsel"
I know the male counterpart

> to girl is boy
> to woman is man
> to lady is lord & gentleman
> to doll & gal is guy

& other uglier terms
but I don't know the counterpart to "damsel"
Still, I'm writing to say that
whatever that counterpart is
I am it
& I am in distress
I am writing to ask for your help
I am writing to ask you to come save me
but I don't need saving from a villain
I sit ensnared in a tangled web
by a hero from a different universe
a Spider-Woman tempting this
fly-by-night &
by-the-seat-of-his-pants artist
to enter her parlor
& stay for dinner
I feel stuck
have tried to break free a couple times
but I fear I can't without
tearing off a pound of flesh from one of us
& I'm trying to not hurt anyone
So, I'm writing to ask you to come save me
but not from her

I'm writing to ask you to come save me

                        from you

See, I'm also ensnared by your lasso &
      truth be told,
                I love you
      truth be told, I love you *both*
I just love *you* for all the right reasons
      not for what you do for me
          but what you do
      not for who you are to me
          but who you are
      not because you need me
      but because you don't
This is what I see, when I look at you
      but looks can be deceiving
          & the grass on the other side
         could be Poison Ivy
All I see is Wonder Woman
      when I don't even know if I ever met Diana
So, I'm writing to ask you
    to come save me
        come down from that pedestal,
          where I placed you
             like a statue of the Greek Gods
        from whence you came
    & stop saving the world long enough
        to save me
              from you
              from your pull
          tearing me apart from myself
            more than from the web
        of the Spider-Woman

to show me that Diana is really Two-Face
because all I see
is the Harvey Dent they want us to see
the ideal of a knight in shining armor
not the scarred, flawed, fallible human underneath
Here I am
trying to fall somewhere between
Superman & Batman
feeling a little more like the Joker
or at least the Batman of another sista's story
The real trouble is just that:
it's all just a story
with all its characters
the heroes
the villains
the victims
the complications
when I need to make it simple
So come down to earth, angel
& show me you're really human
save me from my distress
from you
from love
save me
from myself.

Moon View

Are you there tonight?
Are you really & truly there
　　　or is it just an illusion?
They say you are full
　　　but it's really just a reflection of another's light
The last time anyone visited you
　　　they found nothing but dust & rocks
　　　　　　left nothing but fabric floating weightless
　　　　　　　　　　anchored by metal
　　　　　　　patriotic accessories
　　　　to adorn your heavenly body
　　　　　　symbolizing places places
　　　　　　　　　　you've never been
　　　　　　like a T-shirt
　　　　　　　　keychain
　　　　　　　　shot glass souvenir
　　　　to label you
　　　　　claim you
　　　　　call you theirs
　　　　　own you
　　　　without even getting to really know you
This one-night stand has been immortalized
　　　on media that still sails through the void
　　　　　to civilizations we may never know
　　but will you forget
　　　can you forget
　　would you forget?

If you had air to breath
               to draw in deeps sighs & sobs
        would you cry rain for days
             to wash their red, white & blue stain away
        or do you cherish the memory
               trace moon dust fingers
                   over stars & stripes
               recall what it is to be touched
               relive it nightly?
Do you even remember it
        or was this branding less the bite of tattoo needle
             & more that of a gnat
                   mosquito
                   insect crawling on your skin
             for the relatively briefest of moments
               a second among millennia?
Were we forgotten seconds after leaving
        taking with us pieces of you to feed
             our curiosity
             our imagination
             our egos
        while you carried on your work uninterrupted
             moving our water
             reflecting sunlight
             being there
    really & truly there
             adorned only with the remnants of a dream
                   the footprints of ghosts?
Perhaps we're the ones
    who aren't real.

Junkie Too

Today I awoke to the beep-beep of my alarm
        not the beep-beep of my phone
I looked for your notes in the usual places
        but didn't find any
I wondered if you had nothing to say
        or too much
I wondered if our last conversation
        left more than just your fingers sore
        left a bad taste in your mouth
        left a bad feeling in your heart
I wondered if that last trip was bad
        or if you just had enough of the comedown
                the letdown
                the less than dreamed
                the reality
Today I awoke to find you not there
        no notes in the usual places
        no communication
        no ties
        no tie-offs
        no lines
        no mainlines
        no feeding your addiction
    & I wondered if you were detoxing, too.

The Secret Secret

I have a secret
     about your Secret
     about The Secret
I know why The Secret doesn't work for you
It's because you're trying to make it work for you
    because you're trying to work The Secret
        but there's a secret to The Secret
     & the secret is this:
You can't work The Secret;
     The Secret works you
You can only ride the wave of positive energy
    or crash & drown in your negativity
If you spend your time waiting for your reward
      like waiting for a bus bound for Easy Street
    you're missing the point
     like missing the bus,
        'cause you didn't read the schedule right
The Secret can't reward you
    until you embrace The Secret as its own reward
The journey is the destination
The means is the end
    & you'll never get more
     until you stop asking for more
     until you stop wanting more
       needing more
       missing more
     until you learn to be grateful for all you have
          for all you have

is all that you ever need
except for the knowledge that you have it all
You need to know that you have all that you ever need
before you can ever get more
before you can ever get The Secret to work for you
You need to know it
believe it
feel it
even when it's not enough
Even "not enough" is better than nothing
& no one ever has nothing
Even the poor have their health
Even the sick have their lives
Even the dead have answers we don't
no one ever has nothing
Everyone has something for which to be grateful, so
be grateful
for all that you have
Only then will more come
That's The Real Secret
so, will you listen
or will this Secret secret stay a secret still?

All The Wrong Reasons

I love you
I love the way your hair gets in the way
     when your lips hover over mine
I love the way it falls over your shoulders
      & across your bare breasts
         as you rise up
I love the way you rise up
      rock & roll rhythm hips raising to racing
         wine & grind to wobbly
     big little earthquakes shake to off-balance
         steadied by my hands on your bare breasts
I love the way your breasts look
               fit
               feel in my hands
   the way your skin feels   in my hands
                  on my skin
        smooth & sweaty sliding
     the way your skin looks against mine
        creamy white
               pink in places
            contrasting with my
              seamless tan
              seamless,
           save the scratches down my back
  I love the way you put   scratches down my back
    marking me in a place only I can remember
              a place I can only remember
      why does that hurt?
                    oh, I remember

I love the way that feels
     the way you feel
     the way you feel inside

inside your mouth
your south
your mind
your soul
energy intertwining with tongues & tangled limbs
I love the way you sound
when you say I'm amazing
when you can only say my name
when you can't even say that
when you can't even say anything
ohs echoing from full force
fading to falling whisper
to frozen open mouth
I love the way I can please you like that
the way I can please you over &
over &
over &
over &
over again
the way it pleases me
the way you please me
the way you want to please me
the way you're willing to do whatever
whenever
wherever
however
willing to do nothing whatsoever
to just lay there & hold me
when the spirit is willing but the flesh is weak
or vice versa
I love the way you feel in my arms then
all sighs & resignations
comforting
comforted
comfortable

I love how comfortable you feel in my arms
　　　how comfortable you feel
　　　how comfortable this feels
　　　　　comfortable
　　how

　　　　　you
　love

　　　　this
　　　　　feel
　　　　　　in my
　　　sighs
I love how you love my sighs
　　　　& my size
　　　　& my size
　　　　my shoulders
　　melting as you massage away all the stress
　　　　　except that which I put there over you
　　& how it doesn't matter how you massage
　　　　　to excite or relax
　　　　　to entice or relieve
　　　　you love my reactions
　　　　　& I love that
I love that you look up to me
　　　that I inspire you
　　　　　motivate you
　　　　　move you to want better for yourself
　　　　　　　& from yourself
I love that you think I'm better
　　　that you think about me that way
　　　that you look at me that way
I love the way you look at me
　　　with eyes of crystal
　　　　　starlight reflecting
　　　shining the glow of the halo you perceive
　　　　　adoration tangibly soft as fleece
　　　so full of love
I love that

I love you
     so much
     just enough
         to want someone else for you
            someone who'll return those looks
            someone who looks at you
         the way you look at me
            someone who looks at you that way
         because he loves you
          not someone who loves you
         because you look at him that way
            someone who loves you
         for all the right reasons
         for everything you are
      not just everything you are to him
I want all this for you
     & I want you to want all this for you
I want you to look at yourself
     the way you look at me
         to know you deserve all this
         to know you deserve better for yourself
                 & from yourself
         to know you deserve
             someone else
I want all this for you
     because I love you
         so much
            but only
     so much.

Greek Tragedy

You are a Greek god
      not in form but in function
You look more Buddha than Zeus
      but your words …
Your words are Leda's swan
      all beauty & beastly
      all grace & savagery
      all gentle overpowering
You speak as Homer
      weaving fact with fable
          'til all are too fantastic to believe
      weaving skillfully, like Arachne at a lyrical loom
          daring to boast
          daring to challenge
          daring to win
Your words are the hands of artisans
      carving
      painting
      molding your image into the temples of Word
      forcing your way behind temples &
          deep into catacombs of souls
      scribing into stone
          your place in the annals
          of our modern mythology
          but your actions …
Your actions are an open box
              an undipped heel
              a Gorgon's glance
They are both the stolen flame
      & the beak in the liver
They are the club foot
          the cryptic riddle
          the children of a love unspeakable

They are waters just too low
        fruits just too high
        boulders forever uphill
        worlds forever heavy on shoulders
Your actions are the unforgiveable crime
      & the unending punishment
You were safe in the center of the wide pedestal
      the pillar marked colleague
              mentor
              idol
              friend
              brother
              god
      held up when others tried tearing you down
I got so used to having put you there
      that I didn't notice you were gone
        'til long after you climbed down
              destroyed the pedestal &
              desecrated the temple
        making it cracked & crooked
        making no other idol sit exactly straight
              sit centered
              sit securely
Now, everyone falls off eventually
Your words are still beautifully powerful &
          powerfully beautiful
      like an image of the Gods
        but your actions are like those of the Gods
           selfish, destructive, betraying
        leaving my temple to friendship in ruins
          my trust in the concept
         forever shaken
   & that
      is a tragedy.

Assorted Haiku, Senryū & Tanka

I've decided that
It isn't really that long
A drive to Worcester

> I think I love you;
> I hope you'll give me the time
> I need to be sure.

> > I wish that I could
> > Write about my pain without
> > Holding onto it

> *Broken Mantra*
> I will be patient;
> I will be patient; I will …
> Try to be patient

Oh, I could so win
At a haiku Slam™, just based
On the sheer volume

> You'll never be mine,
> Partly because I am not
> Looking to own you.

> > I'll have the tea kettle
> > Whistle up a wind to
> > Fill my empty sails.

> *Prompts*
> Why should I need prompts
> To inspire daily poems,
> When you're in my heart?

I hate this poem
Because I wrote it for you
& it is **so** good!

I misread the signs;
I shouldn't have tried to drive,
When blinded by love.

Follow the Muse, plainly
I follow the muse,
Go where it takes me; sometimes,
The path leads to you;
Sometimes, it leads to other things,
But it always tells my tale.

Follow the Muse, redux
Following faeries
Down crystal river flowing,
See the doe grazing,
The trees or the mountainside,
Always through my reflection.

I let loose the rain
Of words on the page, hold back
The rain from my eyes;
All I have to say won't fit
In a haiku or tanka.

Sacrilege

Contrary to popular belief,
      I don't think of myself as Caesar
& everyone knows the realm here isn't
      reliving the glory days of Rome
So, I'm not going to kill the messenger,
      but it doesn't mean I have to like the message
I've been told I won't be crucified on my return
& while I hate to substantiate the other belief that
      I see myself as the Providence Jesus
I have to take exception
      to being pardoned like Barabbas
        as if I get a free pass
            on murdering the movement
            when I was just trying to give it life like Lazarus
& while I hate to substantiate the other belief that
      I see myself as the Providence Jesus
I have to point out that I, too,
      had problems at first with being assigned
        the moniker of savior
& while I hate to substantiate the other belief that
      I see myself as the Providence Jesus
I did try to teach *everyone*
      that they were just as capable
            just as powerful
            just as *responsible* as I was
        for the movement's success
               or demise
& I did try to pick the proper people
      to be poetry's apostles &
        continue things long after I was gone

I had no idea that running a reading &

building a community
would become an epic drama
of Biblical proportions
had no idea that everyone was Judas
waiting in line to give me & the movement
the Kiss of Death
had no idea that Mother Mary was already
too much martyr
that the movement couldn't
sustain another
when she had long ago left *vacant*
her cross to bear
or to burn
I had no idea that I
was supposed to carry the weight by myself
supposed to give my body
my blood
my whole life
without voicing hesitation or
reservation or
irritation or
expectation of reciprocation
I didn't know the rock
upon which I tried to rebuild a house of God
was shale
didn't know the house was of real cards
jokers, suicide kings, black queens,
all in the Lonely Hearts Club
putting spades in backs &
serving up aces in holes
trying to draw the 10
Go ahead & tally your points
& count your chips
while the real word of God falls on deaf ears
"You are not the fucking choir"

more like inquisitors
torturing
banishing
murdering innocent J.E.W's
in the name of your God
yourself
& while I hate to substantiate the other belief that
I see myself as the Providence Jesus
I consider this my tantrum at the temple
tossing tables in a tizzy
while people sell their wares

& themselves

Don't get me wrong
I'm not saying this place is so holy
that it's wrong to hock your words here
I'm just saying it'd be nice
if those words actually *meant* something
if their speakers actually *meant* what they spoke
if the audience actually *listened,*
rather than just *heard*
Don't get me wrong
I'm not trying to go against the dogma of
"Judge not, let ye be judged"
I'm just saying that I *have* been judged
inaccurately & unfairly

& it hurts

Don't get me wrong
I'm not trying to be unappreciative
It's nice that I won't be crucified on my return
I'm just trying to say that it'd be nicer still
if I were actually missed.

Spelled Right & Proper

I heart you
I less-than-3 you
I will always wuv you
   because even L-U-V is too close when spoken
The word is hard for me
     hard with anybody
  but especially with you
& what we do is far more than fucking
   but still less than
     less-than-3
    no matter how close we come
       how hard we come
       how much we come
       2.9999997
    just so long as that period is there
We came close to 3 once
   & panicked
We didn't want to go too far
   because we heard 7 8 9
    but knew 3 would devour dreams
        polish off plans
       ravage resources
    & the last time someone made 3 with me
     she made trouble
       took too much of me out
       & too much out of me
       tried to force my round peg
        into her square hole
    the effort left me broken & discarded
      like the childhood toy she played with
      like the dog she abused
      like the love I had for her
  & held me down

held me up
held me back
for years
Now I'm too scared to look
too scared to feel
too scared to know
to let go
to relax into
whatever this is
I'm too scared to even ask whatever this is
this
feeling for you, this
fear of feeling more
& am I even capable of feeling more?
What am I afraid of
failure
or success
or both?
hurting you
or being hurt
or both
or neither?
am I afraid of this being it
being The One
being the end
of just letting this be?
am I too afraid
to just let
this
be?
I am too afraid to just let this be
this isn't good
this isn't right
this isn't
love

at least, not the kind you're thinking of
        not the kind I'm longing for
        not the kind that leaves me
                at a loss for lines
    but the kind where the lines are
              caught in my throat
      not stuck from a feeling too big
        but not enough to push out
      plodding prosodic feet to catch like hooks
No wonder you think something's fishy
    but it's just me being wishy-washy
      waffling in my worry
      wanting more for you
            from me
I want to do more than
      less-than-3 you
      more than even L-U-V you
   but the word just won't come easy to me, anymore
It'll take more than music
   to charm it out of my basket heart
      more than the right chemical reaction
   to induce it out of me
It'll take a real magic spell
    to stir the steam out of my cauldron
      a real fisher queen
   to reel those lines out of my watery depths
    a real love
        L-O-V-E
     spelled right & proper
     with mouth &
        eyes &
        hands &
        every fiber of my being

I don't want to be afraid to use the word
     I want to be afraid to **not** use it
I don't just want to make the word easy
     I want to make it unnecessary
     I want to make it erupt out of me
                   out of every pore
                     every orifice

     emptying me
     rendering me

          speechless.

This Anger

Tonight, I've seen the face of God
                    heard the message God's been
                                   sending me for years
                    heard the warnings of what can happen
                                        if it goes unheeded
        & I flinched
          I closed my eyes
            covered my ears
            shut every sense I could
          I flinched
          I blinked in a staring contest with the Mirror
            balked on the mound with me at the plate,
                                        checking my swing
          I flinched in pain
              slamming feelers in the door of my heart
                  the pain of closing yourself off
                                        from yourself
                    somewhere between stinging
                              between pins & needles
                        & the dull constant ache
                        in the shoulders of my soul
I am tired & sore
        from carrying this weight
                              this 36-ton chip
                              these 36 years
                              this burden of hate is heavy
              but I can't let it go
It is my creation
    my child

I have birthed it from the womb of my poisoned heart
      through holes in me forced open by rape-ier wit
          oozing their seed of self-doubt inside me
             where I can't wash it clean
         then blaming me for being so easy
                 & for not enjoying it
        like it's wrong to complain
Just shut up & take it!
    but I feel plowed over
        turned
      with this diseased kernel sprouting weeds
        destroying the land of my soul
I need to purge myself of this sickness
      release myself from this burden
    but I can't let it go until someone picks it up
It is my creation
   my child
      birthed from the forever-open wounds of my heart
      reaped from the sick seeds sown into my soul
        & I cannot release it into the wild to die
Dammit, someone has to take responsibility for this!
I didn't ask for it
I didn't want it
     but I just can't let it go
      'til someone takes responsibility
            makes restitution
           makes it right!
I just want someone to make it right!
Please, someone make it alright
But no one ever comes
   no one ever claims my child
          my creation
          my burden
          my weight of worthlessness
          my 36-year
            36-ton chip on my shoulder
              chip

It's more like a boulder
        a rock
        a world that's my burden to bear
                my punishment
    for turning from the face of God
    for ignoring the message God's been
                 sending for years
    for being afraid to look in the Mirror
        afraid that I was not Atlas
              not Prometheus
              but Medusa
      afraid that looking in the Mirror
   wasn't looking at God
           but at a monster
     afraid that I would turn to stone
        or was it a different kind of monster
        green
        decaying
        hulking
        lumbering
        lurking
        looking through my eyes
     afraid of the fire that still burns inside me
           the heat
           the light
           the life
           the love that's still there
                    waiting
     to be seen
        heard
        felt
        known
I can still feel it inside
    but I've been taught to not touch
        been burned to scarring
            to seared flesh

been discouraged from running fingers
over lit candles
running feet
over hot coals
had ovens blow in my face
& singe eyebrows
I'm afraid to light incense
for fear of burning this house to the ground
this house where fear lives
in fear

fear of opening the door & letting anyone in
fear of being forced out into the open
fear of being alone
of being surrounded
of being a failure
a success
a fraud
of just being

of being me
There's something wrong with being me
There's something wrong with   me
what's wrong with me?
This is killing me
holding me back
holding me down
keeping me from standing
from growing
from going beyond its boundaries
from being free
Why can't I let this go
when I know it's bad for me to hold on?

How do I forgive & not forget

forgive for me & not for them
forget the pain & not the lesson?
How do I get past my past
& live in the present
for the sake of my future?
I am tired & sore
from carrying this weight
this 36-ton chip
these 36 years
this burden of hate is heavy
& I think I'm finally ready to know
How do I just let this anger

go?

This Is Enough

You taught me how to be hungry
      but do you know how to be full?
You always till the field
      but do you ever reap the fruits of your labor
              feast yourself &
              sit sated?
      do you ever sit?
You are kinetic
      dynamic
      electric
    but do you know the power of stillness?
Silence can be deafening
    to those who will hear it
      if we stop talking long enough
    to hear the words interlaced in our heartbeats
Life is a paradox
    where the journey is the destination
      & the answers lie in questioning
    & God will fill our cups to overflowing
      as soon as we believe that we have plenty
        & we do
                      have
                        plenty
      for we have today
        & today is everything
We wake
    & are already ahead of those who can't wake
      for we have today
    to press on or start over
      we have today

the present
the gift &
the gift of this life
of this air we breathe
this chance we take
to connect
to share
to join
to hold
to embrace
Even someone without arms
can embrace another's heart
embrace new concepts
embrace life
live life to its fullest
live him to his fullness
& feel his fullness
& enjoy it
Can you feel your fullness
or are you always hungry?
Do you love the ache in your muscles
or must you always be dancing
always be moving
& never be moved?
Even the liveliest melody
has a place for the notes to rest
a place just as lovely as when it crests
There is a time for lovemaking
& a time for laying your head on heaving chests
& a time for laying in bed
just as much as for rising & getting dressed
There is value in all this
value that can't be quantified
else it be lost
worth that can't be sold
without selling out

So take your energy & dance free

                                        & enjoy it

  & then sit

    rest

    catch your breath

                                        & enjoy it

Lay your head on your pillow

    to sleep, perchance to dream

  & then wake

  & do it all again

  & know

     this is enough.

Gordium

We tied this "not" around my wrist
  knotted this "not-it" securely around my wrist
    a bracelet to ID what this is & is not
      warning of allergies to bad medicine
        of bad cases of a different kind
 Still my airways are constricted
  a reaction to this fiber
    feeling noose-like around my wrist
"It stretches when wet," you said,
  so we get wet
   & stretch limbs
   & the limits
 of what is & is not
The wetter we get
  the more we stretch our limits
The wetter it gets
  the more I stretch it past digits
    'til it slacks
     slips
     slides right off
It was so easy
  & I was so hard
  & you were so easy
   but this is so hard
  & I was so easy
   but I'm just too hard
  & now it's too easy
   because it's too hard
    too easy to lose
   & too hard to let loose

I'm lost
I'm losing it
I don't want to lose this
       but I'm tied up in this "not"
            I can't undo this "not"
           won't undo this "not"
We tied this "not" around my wrist
       knotted this "not-it" securely around my wrist
            a bracelet to ID what this is & is not
                & this is not "it"
I know this
I know this is not what I want
I just don't want to say it
       for fear that my tongue is a sword sheathed
              & my words are the down-stroke
       to cut ties.

Bring The Birds

Some say I brought fire to you
Others say I put the fire in you
Either way
                  it was I who taught you how to burn
My nephew knew the risks
      & wanted to wash the slate clean
            but I had high hopes
                helped you tread high waters
                taught you how to survive
                        how to thrive
                        to live
                        to light the way
                    for yourselves & others
                  how to burn
            & you have never stopped burning
Whatever is laid in front of you
      you put a flame to it
          even your brother
& when he learned to back away
            out of the reach of your flame
        you learned to throw it
            shoot it
            drop it
            launch it
            fire it from the sky
& when your brother was still standing
        you taught the flame to burn hotter
                  burn brighter
                  burn long after it dies

to be all-consuming

                     to be your echo

                         your reflection

                         your clone

                                   burning from the inside out

                                   destroying all you touch

It's been said that my punishment was

        to have an eagle eat the lobes of my liver

                only to have the liver grow back

                        so that the torture could continue

                                        for all eternity

        but it was enough just to tie me to this rock

                high above the inferno

            forced to witness what you've done

            with my gift to you

Oh, Zeus!

Would that you had sent more

    than just an eagle for my liver!

Would that you had sent a hawk for my heart

                                or magpies for my eyes!

Let me not see this abomination of man

Let me not feel this pain

           this sorrow

           this shame

Let me not feel

Let me be mortal

Let me starve

    & bleed

    & die

Let me die

Let me stay dead

        rather than watch this tragedy play out

            & die a hundred thousand times

Gods, the smell
        the smell of seared flesh
                & scorched earth
Gods, the sound of wailing
      enough to drown my own screams
Gods, the pain
        the pain of this pride turned poison
           irony twisting like a blade in my belly
              worse than this one bird
Oh, Gods!
                    just this one bird?!

Bring a buzzard for *my* beak
      so that I don't have to smell
Bring gulls for my ears
      so that I don't have to hear
Bring a bevy of birds to this Titanic buffet
      to pick my bones clean
Just please
      don't leave me here
      don't make me watch
           hear
           smell
           feel
      don't make me live this
        please
                it burns.

All About Me

It's all about me
That's what you said
      & I could tell part of you was joking
             but not which part
                   or how much
     & I was hurt
              hurt by your casual sarcasm
              hurt by such a shallow image of me
              hurt by the truth
It *was* all about me
    is all about me
    & will be, 'til I say it's not
            'til I want it to be about someone else
            'til I think I can handle it
      which is not right now
Don't misunderstand me
I'm not saying I don't care
     but this isn't love
          nor is it the beginnings of
It's about exploration
          experimentation
     or at least sufficient distraction
         in the guise of physical attraction
I read while I write & I cringe at my own words
                at my own cruelty
                at my own insensitivity
                at my own reality

I know this will hurt to hear
   more than it hurts to say
  but we must prepare for the day
    when we must rewind this love scene
  to the friendship from whence it came
    & pause
But will it pause forever
  staying focused on the friendship image
   or will it blur
     fade away
     deteriorate from overuse?
I fear it's already time too soon
      time to find out
I fear I already know the answer
  is not the one I want
I fear the pain I might cause
  & there is very little
    but hopefully enough consolation
   in the fact that, before we even started,
    you knew where my head was at
    you knew where I was coming from
    you knew what I wanted from this
    you knew
      it was all about me.

If I Could Only Reach
[a poem with a twist]

The blades of my shoulders
      are the harness & frame
           for the blade of my tongue

                        my mouth
                        my words
                                "I trust you."

Words dull, even soft, to the touch
      but they can still cut deep

                    tear apart a heart & soul

          when used properly
            or improperly,
            depending upon one's perspective
You used those words to do just that
You took that trust & thrust it in my back
      between the blades
      just out of reach
         out of control
Yet, despite the cuts you've made between us
      we are still connected
      we are still vines
                lives intertwined on the same fence
                  chained together by one single link
She is the tie that binds our wrists together
Her love
         our common ground upon which we stand
                            but ...

If I could only reach that dagger
      I would use it to sever all ties with you
                cut your cord, if I could,
        to her
        to me
        to us
           forever

If I could only reach that dagger
    I'd remove it from my back
        & let the wound finally start to heal
    I'd use it to rip your heart from your chest
        & let it bleed on the floor of this stage
            that was once the pedestal
        where I placed you
Maybe if I could only reach
        if I could only remove the knife from my back
            the thorn from my side
            the pain from my heat
            the aching in my soul
Maybe I could just let it go
        let it fall to the floor
        close that door
      worry me no more
    & not let my anger drive me to acts of revenge
But the blade is buried between my blades
    just out of my reach
& the situation is out of my control
So I must live with the pain of this betrayal
            of this uncertainty
    wait for gentle hands that,
        despite all assurances otherwise,
      won't deny the possibility
    that they may never come
      to remove the blade
      heal my wounds
        relieve me of this painful burden I bear
        a buarden I would not carry
            'tween my shoulders
        if I could only reach …

& waiting,
    there's the *twist.*

Off The Pot

I went to a witch
       in search of a little magic
              only to find myself reacting badly
                     to the compounds in her potions
                     to the visions they induce
                        the past is
                        the present is
                        the future vision
   & I know it's not her
              not her fault
      I know it's me
                         my body chemistry
              altered by traces of past pollutants
                     by my preexisting conditions
                 complicating these seemingly simple things
     but I can't help the vomiting
              the puking up &
                   purging the past
                                into her porcelain
           when she's already dealing with her own shit
How then am I the one
       feeling clogged
            blocked
            stopped up
            unable to flush the past
                & fill with this clean, pure love?
How then can I flush the past
      without flushing the love?
How can I take any more of her potions
      without the past coming back up
      without the shit coming out
      without Montezuma taking his revenge
                          on my heart?

How can the past keep coming up
        the shit keep coming out
    when I've purged myself to feeling empty?
How can we begin to clean up
    when I keep making a mess of my emotions?
How can I begin to heal
        to feel better

                about this

    when I keep making myself sick
        switching from sitting & squirting
           to on sore knees hurling
      but always doubled over in pain
        always crouching in fear?
It's not her
  not her fault
  not her water
  not her potions
Perhaps it's something in the air
          in the fumes hanging
              about her cabin
Scent is the sense tied closest to memory
    & the smells
      sights
      sounds
          are all too much like the past
      for her spells to ever truly work

I need to get up from her porcelain
    & walk off this pain
        until I'm strong enough to work my own magic
          from inside me
    & let her save her potions
      for someone who can stomach them.

The Same Voice

Old friend
Respected colleague
Kind spirit
Keep your eyes on the bobblehead in my car
It sits not on the dashboard
  but in the driver's seat
  inhaling your exhales like exhaust
   strong enough to fuel my engine
  handing out validation
   like candy on Halloween
    or change to homeless
     small
     insignificant
     throwaway gifts to strangers
    hoping you'll appreciate & enjoy it responsibly
     but not emotionally invested enough
      in the banks of minds
     interest not growing beyond now
Don't misunderstand me
I appreciate the advice &, to some extent, you're right
  like, to some extent, you mostly are
       about most things
        most of the time
   but all your talking makes me wonder
    if you're truly listening
    if you're truly hearing me
     seeing me
     knowing me
     getting me
Yes,
  I do use the same voice to soothe my son
   that I use to seduce a woman
No,

I do not do poems that say,
    "Luke, I love you"
    with the same voice I use to say,
        "Woman, I want to fuck you."
How can both be true,
    when they seem to be opposites?
Because they're not
See, it's been a long time since I've written
        never mind read
    a poem to a woman
        about simple fucking
I use the same voice
    because I speak from the same place
            a place of light
      where the darkness in me isn't afraid to go
      where the shadows play & revel
          not only in their existence
           but in the knowledge of the fact that they
             are cast by such a wonderful light
            a place of love

      real
      pure
      unadulterated
      unwavering
                   love
The voice I use to soothe my son
The voice I use to seduce a woman
    is the same voice I'm using to reach you now
Old friend
Respected colleague
Kind spirit

Put down your whisky
        & invite your demons to tea
           take them for walks on the beach
           play with them in open fields
           marvel at how unafraid they are of the sun
           watch them soften in your warm embrace
Dare to speak to a grown woman
        with the same voice you use to soothe your little girl
Dare to believe yourself worthy of love
        & to use the same voice
           with yourself.

Dear Frankenstein
(or What Passes For Art)

Blood red
Semen creamy
Dip tongue brush in orifices natural & self-made
Vomit poisoned pollack on paper
      & fashion yourself a Pollock
Squeeze out your loaf of brown clay
Mold it & put it on display
Will you use special oils to take the smell away
        or will you just smile & say
              it's part of the art?
So many string guitars with overgrown pubic hairs
             diseased toe nails as picks
      & demand we cry
        like we just heard the Black Venus
                or a Jimi riff
I cry like canine too close to siren call
      like cat with tail caught under clogs
      like momma come home from third job
          struggling to pay for baby's better life
              come home to see
                    baby's better life
             oozing onto the concrete
                    baby's better life
          collaterally caught in cop-crook crossfire
I cry for the death of real art
I cry for the walking corpse in its place
I cry for the villagers not running *away* in terror
      but *forward*
              & not in *fury* with fires & forks pitched
      but in *adoration*
         calling creature Christ
            or at least Lazarus

not the shambling shambles of sincerity
it truly is
I hunt the monster
the *real* monster in this story
the creator of what passes for art
the Van Gogh-cum-Frankenstein
as the creature hunts the Victor
but not to destroy
but to *find* everything he loves
to dip his hands in his chakras
teach him to grope the canvas
like a lover
like a blind man
feeling blank pages for the Bible in Braille
searching for the last semblance of truth
left in his soul
I am on my knees to him,
like he were the God he plays at
begging
pleading
praying he resurrect that part of him that *is* God
reconnect &
recreate that for us all to not just witness
but *live* through the work
& if you think I'm not talking about you
then I just might be
& if you think I *am* talking about you
… I *still* might be
but at least you hear me
Let this Rhode Island Red crow your wakeup call
Let this verse be your reveille

Don't just cum
       cry
       sweat
       shed
       shit
       piss
       puke
       bleed on the page
                stage
                stone
                canvas
                track
                film
Die on it
Make me die with you
Bring us all
          to life.

The Lie & The Slap

She tells me she has only two rules:
   "Never lie to me
  & never hit me"
  & I've never done either
           technically
  but there are corners of myself I closed off so hard
    that they jammed
      stuck
    & now I can't open them for all my effort
       not that I'm trying all that hard
There are dark corners of shame
  wolfish shadows that swallow light whole
    & wash it down with sips at my soul
There are corners of light so brilliant
  the edges of the blazing brightness a blade
    to slash through shadow skin
      & set free a love cloaked in vibrant red
  but bits of it have been shared before
      used before
      lost before
    the blades turned against me
     cutting at my soul
     making slices safer for shadows to swallow
     making smaller pieces easier to steal
  these diamond edges deemed
   too precious to be shared again
There are corners corroded
   corrupted
   cracked & crumbling
  pieces sold to the highest bidder
   like the Berlin Wall
  pieces given away
   like candy on Halloween

pieces I'm so used to sharing with everyone
whether or not I should
that I don't know how to save them
for only one
Yes, there are all sorts of corners
& then there's the core
the center
the sacred self
closed off
cloaked
masked & hidden away for so long
I'm not sure what it looks like, anymore
Is it a monster
a hideous abomination
a shameful reminder of past perversion
waiting to be slain
or a man,
made ugly by vindictive witches
looking to teach lessons in morality?
Is it a man shut away from everyone
just waiting for the right woman
to love him human again?
If so,
why isn't this enough
to blow all the doors wide open to every wing
& take the wild animal façade off me?
Which is the façade:
the animal or the man?
Which is the true me
& which is the lie?
Does it still count as a lie,
if I can't tell which is true?
She said, "Never hit me
& never lie to me

& I've never done either, technically,
        but there are corners
        & there's the core
                there are parts of myself I'm not sharing
                        parts that are
                                    hidden from everyone
                        parts that are
                                        given to everyone
                        parts that are
                                reserved for that special one
        her name carved in my stone heart
                only clear enough
            to tell what it's not
                becoming clearer
            with every miss
                                every misstep
                                every mistaken identity
                                every mistake
Not to call this both cosmic & carnal connection
                                                    incorrect
            this ethereal & erotic ecstasy
                                an epic error in judgment
        but this beautiful best friendship
                                with unbelievable benefits
            is just that
            is nothing more
            is not The One
What's worse is that I can see the next one coming
                                can feel her coming closer
                                        with every step
                                can hear her name echoing
                                            in my soul
        & I find myself hoping that
            I've finally found the match to my inscription

That's the real secret
     the rose under the glass
     the face under the mask
     the part of me I'm too afraid to share
How can I dare?
How can I open all of this
          all of me to her
   without tearing her down?
Now that she's falling
     how can I just let her go
        let her drop
        let her break on the surface of
            the harsh, cruel world?
How can I break my best friend's heart?
How can I not break my promise
     to not break her rules?
She said, "Never hit me
     & never lie to me"
   & I've never done either
         technically
   but there are parts of myself I'm not sharing
    & this omission feels like a lie
     but the truth
         feels like a slap in the face.

The End Of Forever

I am here
I have always been here
I will always be here
    as people randomly walk by
                walk in & out of view
    as people purposely walk
              run
              job briskly by
    as people stop to rest
              lean
              stretch
    as people sit under my shade
         carve 4-EVA into my skin
         dream of the word meaning something
    as people climb my limbs
         with their limbs
      giving no thought to what the word means
    as people come
    as people go
      giving no thought to me
I am here
I have always been here
I will always be here
    from the moment of first light
      my seed waiting for the first rain
    to the moment of harvesting knowledge forbidden
    to the moment of forgetting
      memories falling from minds like leaves
    to the moments replayed
      round & round like rings
    to the moment of darkness
      covering all like a blanket of winter
      bringing forever to utter irrelevance

Forever
Forever is just a heartbeat
                    a heartbreak
                    a heart bounding
          it is a sneeze
                    a sigh
                    a scream to lungs empty
          it is a dream
                    a vision
                    a memory
                    a regret
                    an afterthought
          it is a blur
                    a breath
                    a breeze
                    a blink of an eye
          it is nothing in the nothingness
                    a single tear in an ocean storm
                    a whisper in its hurricane winds
                    a flash of its lightning
                              & it's gone
Forever is just a moment
                              & it's gone
          just as now is already then
                    before the word is out of your mouth
Forever is just another word out of your mouth
          & you dream of it meaning something
                    but what do you know of forever
                                                  of meaning
                                                  of dreams?

what do you know?
			you
					are just a moment
		& gone
			you do not know
				can not know
			have not known
			have not seen
			have not been
							here
		as I have been				here
		as I will be				here
	to the end of things
		the end of words
		the end of meaning
		the end of forever
long after the end
			of you.

Leaving The Game

It's hard to tell who's black & who's white
      in this game
It's hard to tell who made the first move
              the first attack
              the first capture
              the first play for the queen
It's hard to tell when this game even started
It's hard to remember how we got this far into it
         how we lost so many pieces
Nevertheless, here we are
      two kings
          each with a single pawn
             waiting to move
             waiting to think
             waiting to breathe
In chess, a situation like this would call for either a draw
      or a concession
A draw is when both players can make
      10 distinct & different moves
         without landing in checkmate
A concession explains itself
An honorable player allows his opponent
      to claim the role of victor
         & leaves the game
So, the obvious question is, of course,
      what happens next?
Which one of us has the option to move next,
      & which move will that person make?
Should we go for the draw & hope for the kill?
Should we go for the kill & hope for... something?
      or should one of us...
No, let's not avoid the issue

Should *I*
     lay my king down
     shake your hand
        & walk away?
A real chess game
       would find me taking sage advice easily
    but a real chess game
      never had such high stakes
        as the love of this queen
I'm so afraid to give her up to you know;
I can't give her up now,
     after everything we've been through
But I'm so afraid to move
        afraid of your next move
        afraid to lose
   & when you become too scared to play the game
       it stops being fun
        stops being healthy
        stops being
              worth it
In battling to get back my queen,
      I've lost all my other pieces
   & as much as it hurts to admit defeat,
      I've got to stop playing games
       & live my life

Congratulations,
    & good luck.

These Apologies

I'm sorry you had a crush
    when I felt only lust
I'm sorry you felt magic
    when I felt only a strong chemistry
       & a touch of hope
I'm sorry you saw sparks
    where I saw only potential
       & an acceptable compromise
I'm sorry I made you fall in love
    when you only made me feel loved
          appreciated
          understood
          safe
        & comfortable
I'm sorry I shut you out
    when you were opening yourself to me
I'm sorry I see the same old patterns for myself
    in something you've never had before
I'm sorry I see in someone else
    what you saw in me
       I feel for someone else
    what you felt for me
       I want with someone else
    what you wanted with only me
I'm sorry you feel that you have nowhere else to turn
    when my options seem limitless
       & when I feel I can always turn to myself
I'm sorry you feel that you can't turn to yourself
    when I tried so hard to make you feel worthy

I'm sorry I have to undo all that work
       when I'm just trying to be honest
          with us all
I'm sorry I broke your heart
       when you helped heal mine
I'm sorry you gave me all you had
       & all I can give you now
          are these apologies.

Beware Of Dogs

There were signs
There were fences
There were long & winding roads to my front steps
There were more signs
There were walls
There were the foreboding tones of my doorbell
    the low growl from my throat
    the scared look on my face
You reached out not to pet
      but to grab by the collar
   & drag home to wear your husband's pants
But I was not made to put on that costume
     to walk on two legs
     to play that role of
       George to your Mary

I was never one to heel
   lie down &
   stay
  never one to obey
I was made to stray
    at least, back in *that* day
  & everyone *knew* it was that way
  & everyone *told* you to stay away
     to *run* away with no delay
    but for all *my* lack of training
     you're the one who didn't listen
You reached into my shelter cage
  looking to own me
    control me
    train me
    make me beg for your treats

Now you act the victim of a mauling
      when all I've *ever* done to *anyone* is snap
      when *your* snaps where *far more* vicious bites
      when you did *far more* than just snap
You tore at scars not yet fully healed
      then dug deeper
You used words
         & eyes
         & hands
         & fists
         & feet
         & tables
         & doors
         & glass
         & lies
         & courts
I used words
      & words
      &   words
You raised your weapons
I raised my voice
      & *I'm* the menace
         the monster
         the mongrel needing to be locked away
                  to be put down
      but I'm tired of this shelter I built for myself
         protecting & caging me at once
I'm finally ready to let someone in
             let someone reach for me
                someone looking to pet me
                  but not looking for a pet
                someone looking for
                      a companion

but I'm scared
 I'm scarred from your abuse
 I'm as lost
 as when I got here
 & I don't know how to find home
 how to take down the cage

the walls

the fences

the signs
 how to heal the wounds you left
 when you mauled me
 simply for acting
 in what was my nature
You shouldn't have gone looking for a dog
 to do a man's job
 to be *your* owner
 to pet
 to protect
 to provide for
 to care for *you*
You shouldn't have gone blaming a dog
 for being a dog
 when *you're* the one who didn't know how to listen
You shouldn't have gone kicking a dog
 again
 when you really wanted to kick yourself
 again
Tell me,
 what does that make you?

Goddess

I am dreaming
I am dreaming of swimming beyond stagnation
                         beyond weight & density
                         beyond darkness
                           swimming into sunlight
                                    into crisp, clean air
            of breathing deep & basking long
I am dreaming of crawling out of murky waters
            of crawling over rough terrain
            of coming up from crawling
I am dreaming of standing upright
            of using tools
            of building something everlasting
I am dreaming of making language
              making art
              making meaning in my life
I am dreaming of going farther
                  faster
                  higher
            of touching the sky
                    the moon
                    the stars
                    the face of God
I am dreaming of being better
              being more
              being worthy
                    of you
                        Goddess

You are a hero to many
     but your powers are far beyond Marvelous fiction
No witch's potion
No chemist's concoction
    can match the sorcerous power you wield
       a magic from deep within you
       a magic I long to learn
           long to touch
           long to feel
           long to be
         I long to be inside you
                   in every way imaginable
                to know how you glow
                   how you go on
       thru the muck of this physical world
         to blossom on all levels
       thru the harshest of weather
       thru all weather
         changing the weather
         showing your awesome power
         Storming the world
         flying Phoenix high
              so that your tribe calls you
                what you truly are
                     Goddess

Goddess of the Struggle
Goddess of the Hunt
Goddess of the Storm
      of the Flame
      of the Light
      of Peace &
        Life &
        Beauty &
             everything

  Goddess

Let me in
Let me in you
Let me know you
Let me learn from you
        touch the magic in you
        learn to make the magic in me
Let's make magic together
        save the world in true hero fashion
        save each other
        save ourselves
        save me
        rescue me from my own darkness
                        my own weight
                        my own density
                        my own stagnation
            help me up thru my own muck
            help me evolve
            help me stand
                    & build
                    & fly
            help me touch the face of God
                        become God
                        become worth

                                        of you

Let me touch your face

                                        Goddess

I know I am not yet worthy to receive you,
        but only say the word
                & I shall begin to heal.

My Move

The wolf in me
    wants to ravage you
        run teeth & tongue along neck bone
            breast bone
            hip bone

      taste your flesh
      swallow you
    but every meal wolfed down
      just leaves me feeling emptier
The explorer in me
    yearns to climb the Aztec temple of your body
      search every catacomb
      worship at your altar
    but past loves have fallen
          grown sick & died away
          become extinct from my
            conquistador ways
      leaving no signs of civilization
The player in me
    is eager to score
       touch down
       split your uprights &
       drive it up your middle
    but every time I rush
      I get sacked
        turned over
        shut out
        & I'm tired of dropping the ball
I've never taken it slow before
    never taken the race at a steady pace before
      & I long to go the distance
        reach the never-finish line
          for once

this promise of forever
                    a winter stream frozen solid in my throat
              from the bitter cold of the knowledge
                 that spring may never come
How can I promise you forever
      when neither of us is promised even tomorrow?
Where is the middle ground
      between living in the now
          & making this moment last?
What do I really want out of this?

                             you
                        just you
I   want   you
                             so much

      but I want to do this right &
      I don't know what's right
Do I repeat rushing the romance & risk ruining it
      or do I take my time & tempt fate
                       to take one of us away?
Do we fuck like bunnies or stroll like turtles?
Do we mate like swans or like dogs in heat?
Which is the right move?
What's my next move?
Why can't I just move?
Why ***don't*** I just
          move?
The world is always turning
To stand still is to move backwards
To make progress
      you have to move
         I have to move
         I ***want*** to move

not stand statuesque as stone unfeeling
forever frozen in fear
let me not fear
let me feel
let me free
let me move
fast or slow, just
move

So, here it is,
my move …
I love you
Now, it's your move
I'll let you
pick the speed.

Rain Dance

I'm dancing naked 'round the fire I burn for you
    & calling
      singing
      praying for your Storm to come my way
I know I could never hope to hold the thunder
I'm just hoping that your cloud will rain on me
      as it passes by.

Still
(If You Let Me)

The world hasn't stopped
Life as we know it still exists
People still walk the earth
      & I haven't changed
          haven't lost my sense
          haven't numbed myself to my surroundings
I still see other people
  still see other women
    smell other women
     feel other women
   want other women
      & it bothers me
              unsettles me
              makes me doubt myself
                      doubt my love
                          my readiness
                          my worthiness
  I feel unworthy of you still
        unworthy of you more than before
        & I second-guess whether I should even
           tell you how I feel
        but it's been said that a sure sign of one's sanity
           is calling it into question
    so can the same be said for this?
If every glance at another woman
        makes me worry about being worthy of you,
           do I really have anything to worry about?
If every longing for another woman
        makes me long for the distraction *of* you,
           am I really distracted *from* you?

Every time I check out another woman
        I check myself
    & not because I *have* to
        because I *don't* have to
    but because I *want* to
We have no agreement
        spoken or otherwise
    but what need have I for
                meaningless sex with others,
        when the memory of your kiss sends me flying
        when the thought of your touch gives me chills
        when the image of just holding you
                completes me?
How can any other compete with that
        compare to you
        coerce me from this course?
Nothing comes close
Though my eye may wander
    my heart
    my head
    my cause isn't lost on lust for the lesser-than
This fantasy isn't based on fantasy
This love is realer than reality
    offering stability not only outside of
        but *through* all temptation
So the world doesn't stop
So life doesn't end
So my hormones don't shut off
So you're not the only woman in the world … so what?
    you're the only one in my heart

So, let the others still come
   let me still see
       still sense
       still smell
       still want them
  I will still love you
         & that will be enough
   let me still lust
       still admire
       still not change
  I will still love you
         & that will stay my hand
   let the world still spin
   let life march on
     I will still
       & always
          love you
                 if you let me.

Do-Over

Let me write you a poem
Let me draw with pencil lead
    sunrises &
    rainbows &
    sunsets more vivid than any painting
        draw portraits of you more beautiful
    than any sunrise or
        rainbow or
        sunset
Let me rehearse a couple dozen times
        in front of a couple dozen people
    & those pictures will flow fast & freely
          frame by frame from my lips
            telling the story of my heart on the big screen
              of minds
      those words will fly off my runway tongue
                   soar through the air &
                   land on the strip of your ear
        the message cabbing it home to your heart
Let me get a moment alone with you, though
Let me have this chance I've been waiting
               wishing
               praying to take

    & I will skip
        stutter &
        stop
        like you're playing my CD in your car
            while driving on New England roads
              after a long, hard winter

I am not good at this
                        at making the first move
                        at opening myself up to more pain
                        at talking about how I feel
        when I feel it
                        so strongly
I'm so used to going with what I know I can get
        because it comes for me first
                but not now
                        not anymore
That road has just led to heartbreak
        too many times for me &
        too many others *by* me
Besides, you inspire me to do the things that scare me
        you inspire me to be **more** afraid of fear
        you inspire me to be **not** afraid to love
        you inspire me to love
        you inspire me
        & that's just some of the reasons why I love you
So, please pardon the
                                pauses &
                f-f-forgive the flubs
        but I'm flustered
                I'm full of feeling for you
                        & I just had to let you know
                        I wanted to let you know
                        I wish I could let you know
                                        better
                        I wish I could have that night back
Let me   have that night back
Let me tell you
better

Let me paint those sunrises &
    rainbows &
    sunsets with my words
Let them fly off my tongue & to your heart
Let me be with you
     as smooth as I am in front of others
Let me have that night back
Let me do this over
Let me write you a poem
   give you a poem
   love you a poem
Let me love you
      please
Let me.

Burn For You

Your touch
Your simple touch
     simple & pure
          with no thoughts of where they could lead
               no intention outside of connection
    connected with me
Your soul
      spoke to my soul
Your windtalker spirit
      spoke the code to unlock my rib cage
      setting free the wild horses I held back in my heart
         for fear of being dragged away by them again
      teaching them to run off my high-board tongue &
              soar Pegasus-like through the air
        enjoying the freefall
        expecting
        hoping
        thirsting to take the plunge
          into the refreshing
              inviting
              safe waters of you
           only to find the pool almost as dry
            as the pages these steeds
                  words
                  feelings
         are written on
It's OK

Your heart is elsewhere
I understand
      & I'm trying to deal
           trying to say your name
                      without too much love pouring out
               like the waterfall that sometimes pours out
                            from my eyes
              just from thinking about
                      never being with you
        trying to hug you
without holding on too long
                    without letting touches linger
        trying to stay satisfied
                 with pecks on the cheek
         knowing how pecks on the lips feel
        trying to see potential in others
             see their light shining
        & not how dim they are
                  when compared to your starlight
     I'm trying to deal
        but it's hard, when my heart still
        sings &
        skips at &
        sighs &
        signs your name all over these pages
            your name
        not some mysterious everywoman
        not a blank to fill with whomever's around
            your name
        etched in this stone sent to cracking
           revealing it to be a casing
                not solid through & through
                      a shell

like its master …
its servant
a wall of protection
of persecution
of pride & pain
sent to crumbling
sent to bursting
setting free these words
to run like wild horses
all over these pages
I thought I was leading them to water
but your signs say clearly that your pool
forms on someone else's property
& my words die of thirst
on the dry landscape of this page
the water from my eyes only *fueling* the fire
of this funeral pyre
These words were brought out by you
put there for you
given to you
meant for you
& you don't want them
Your heart is elsewhere
I understand
but don't tell me to save them
to give them to someone else
as if just anyone else could wear them
These are undergarments
tailored for you
personal
intimate
to be worn close
not just old coats to be given to good will
fit to keep just any body warm

I made them for you
I meant them for you
I feel them for you
If you don't want them,
        I may as well take a match
                        set a wildfire
                                across these arid conditions
            & just let them burn
                            burn them down
                            burn them out
            just as I still burn
                                for you.

Flower

Some acorns grow into mighty oaks
        only because a squirrel forgot where he buried them
    …to put it another way …
Some nuts are forgotten, even by the rodents
     & still grow into tall, strong things
        deeply rooted in the ground
        touching the sky
        breathing life into the air
           lush &
           sturdy &
           safe enough for some to call
                      home
              if they call it   home
              if they have in their animal languages
                a word with which to label
                  this idea
                  this ideal
                  this feeling   home
              if they have
                  this feeling
                      home
& if they have this feeling "home"
       then they must know the feeling of lost
           as we take their down to build ours
           as we foreclose
               repossess
              rip out & destroy
           these pieces of their lives
           as if they're ours to take

What are their words for us?
Do they know our given names
      or do they give us names in their languages?
Would those names translate to something like

                                          Katrina
                                            Rita
                                              Ike
                                          Bob?

      & what, in turn, would they then call the wind storm
          blowing their house in
          blowing the tree to falling in the forest?
If no one is there to hear it,
          does it make a sound?
If no one is there to *see* it,
          is it still a tree
      or do even the trees
         have different words for themselves
            that we're just not trained to hear?
What do they all call themselves?
Puffy yellow blossom bursts forth puffy white seed
        to plant in open fields
        to burst forth more puffy yellow blossom
You call it weed
        but the eyes of a child behold a flower

                            a wonder
                            a thing of beauty
                                    of magic

               for making wishes
                 closing eyes
                 blowing windy kisses
                               …

If a flower grows in an open field
      & no child is there to see it,
         is it still beautiful?

If a weed grows in a sidewalk crack
                              or in your front yard
              & no child is there to call it flower,
                    is it still beautiful?
Is beauty in the eye of the beholder?
Is it all just here for the benefit of others?
Are we all defined
                              by what is perceived of us from the outside?
I know that many see me as a tree or a flower
              but I am a weed to others
My roots may give nourishment or shelter to some
              but some can't get past the bitter taste
                    while others would be poisoned
              yet I still grow
                    still blossom
                    still burst forth everything I am
                    still plant seeds in the fields &
                                    lawns &
                                    sidewalks of your minds
              I still am
              still live
                    no matter what name they call me
                              how they see me
                              how they use me
I stay rooted in the ground
                              & dare to stretch toward the sky
You may now look at your sidewalk crack
              in your bad part of a bad town
                    being ignored by some
                              while others try to rip you out
              & you may wonder where you came from
                    how you got here
                    what you did to deserve this life
                              whether or not you're beautiful

but don't let your surroundings
   dictate your worth
      spray poison on your life &
      kill your soul
  hold fast to your roots
      & stretch as high as you can
If beauty is in the eye of the beholder,
    then I want you to look in the mirror
     with the eyes of a child
       with magic & wonder
          call your reflection

                  flower

      & never

         ever

                    stop growing.

About the poet

JASON E. "JAY" WALKER is from Rhode Island, a state too small to really give too much thought to which city/town/region he's from. He's been writing poetry—mainly spoken word & haiku/senryū—since high school & getting naked in public, figuratively & literally, since 1993. He's a three-time finalist for the original Providence Poetry Slam® team, making first alternate the third time in '98 or '99 (he can't remember which); he's also hosted a few poetry readings in his home state. His first two chapbook publications sold out of their first printings. This is his third official publication & his second with Merry Blacksmith Press.

He has one son, who lives in Massachusetts & has wanted to be an architect, a firefighter, a pyrotechnician & a starting pitcher for the Boston Red Sox, but also has some great dance moves … yes, the boy's name *really is* Luke Sky.

ALSO BY JAY WALKER
FROM MERRY BLAKSMITH PRESS

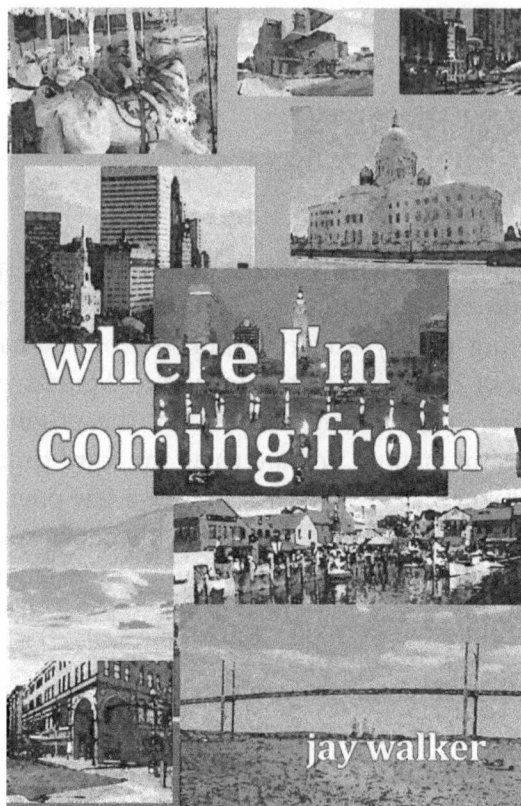

Jay Walker is reaching out to the world through his poetry, speaking on world issues and reflecting on all the aspects & events of his life and his art. *Where I'm Coming From* is not a love letter to Rhode Island; it's a declaration of the status of his emotional journey to the ultimate destination of peace, love & nakedness for all.

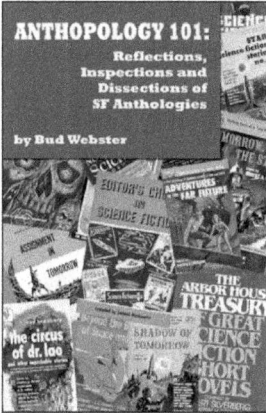

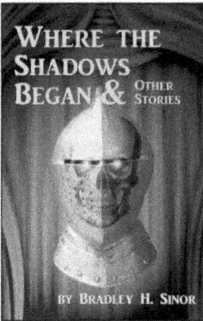

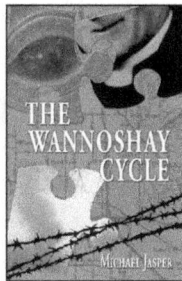

www.ingramcontent.com/pod-product-compliance
Lightning Source LLC
Chambersburg PA
CBHW062004040426
42447CB00010B/1900